WHAT MAKES IT WORK?

Contents

Written by Steve Cunningham

Introduction

Have you ever wondered how an airplane stays in the air? Or how people can talk to each other over such long distances by telephone? What about how a battery or a CD works?

Some inventions operate using basic technology. Others use intricate systems that took a long time to develop. One thing is for sure – all these things were invented because people saw a need for them. They were designed to make life easier, and they all do.

erosol

Eric Rotheim invented the aerosol spray over 75 years ago. A product in an aerosol could be fly spray, paint, or even cooking oil. So, how does an aerosol work?

An aerosol spray contains two liquids. One liquid propels another liquid out of the can. The liquid that propels the other liquid is stored under a higher pressure. This high-pressure liquid is the propellant. The propellant boils below room temperature. The other substance, such as fly spray, boils at a higher temperature. Boiling causes a liquid to turn into a gas. Boiling can happen at different temperatures. The propellant is stored above the product in most aerosol sprays. When you push the spray nozzle down, a valve is released. The propellant then forces the product up a small hose and out of the nozzle. When you release the nozzle, the valve closes. The propellant and the product are then separated again.

Aerosol technology was not popular when it was invented. Now it is used every day. Some propellants harm the environment. Many manufacturers have now replaced these harmful substances.

How an Aerosol Works

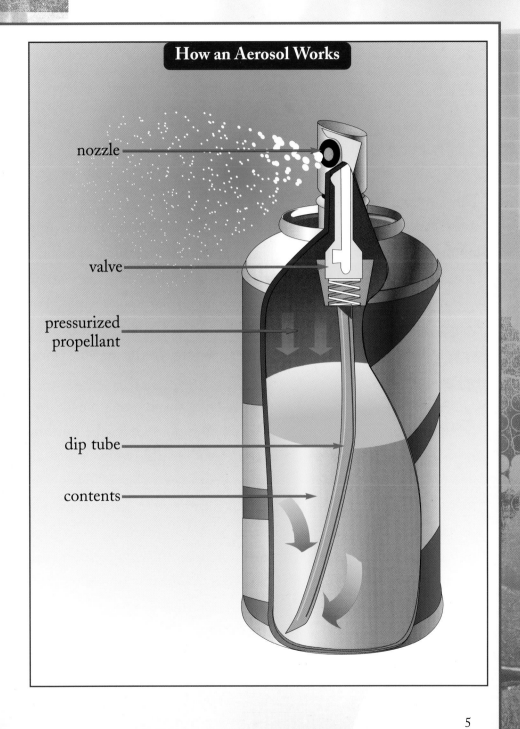

nozzle

valve

pressurized propellant

dip tube

contents

irplane

The airplane is a great feat of engineering. One question that is always asked about airplanes is, "How can something that weighs hundreds of tons stay in the air?" It is amazing something so big and heavy does not fall out of the sky. So, how does an airplane work?

Probably the most important part of an airplane is its wings. The design of the wings allows an airplane to fly. The top part of each wing is curved. The bottom part is flat. To stay in the air, "lift" must be generated.

How is "lift" created? Air travels a longer distance and faster over the curved top of an airplane's wings than it does under the bottom, flat part. The fast air going over the top of the wing causes air pressure to drop. So, the air pressure above the wings is lower than the pressure under the wings. It is this difference in air pressure that causes an airplane to have lift. It then becomes airborne. An airplane has to create a lot of speed for this to happen. A big airplane has to create more speed than a small airplane to get the same amount of lift. Once in the air, an airplane's tail flaps allow it to turn.

Flight has made the world seem like a smaller place. Instead of taking weeks or months to reach somewhere, it now takes only hours or days. It took Christopher Columbus ten weeks to sail from the Canary Islands to the Bahamas. Today that trip would only take hours, thanks to the invention of the airplane.

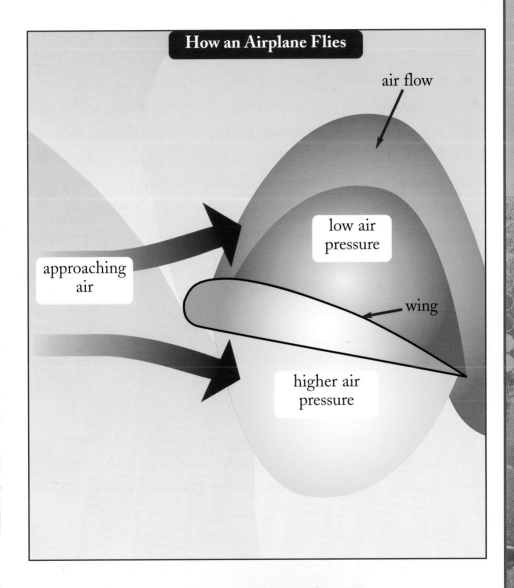

How an Airplane Flies

air flow

approaching air

low air pressure

wing

higher air pressure

attery

Created by Alessandra Volta in 1800, batteries help with many things. Batteries power flashlights, radios, portable tools, and remote controls. A battery is useful because it produces an electrical current. The current means a lot of things can be powered without being plugged into an electrical socket. So, how does a battery work?

Inside a battery there are two electrodes and one electrolyte. An electrolyte produces a chemical reaction with the two electrodes. This in turn produces electrons. The electrons make up the current. The current is what creates the power for things to work.

All batteries have a negative terminal and a positive terminal. The electrodes collect at the negative terminal. If you were to put a wire from the negative terminal to the positive one, all the electrons would travel from the negative terminal to the positive terminal. This creates a circuit, or power. However, connecting a wire from a negative to a positive terminal uses up the power of the battery quickly. This is why a load is introduced. A load is what uses the electricity. A load can be a motor, a light bulb, or a remote-control device. They are powered by the battery.

Batteries help people do things that would otherwise be hard to do. For example, you cannot take electric lights with you when you go on a camping trip. Batteries can be used to power a lantern. If you want to listen to a football game on the radio and you are outside with no electrical outlets, a battery will allow you to power a radio.

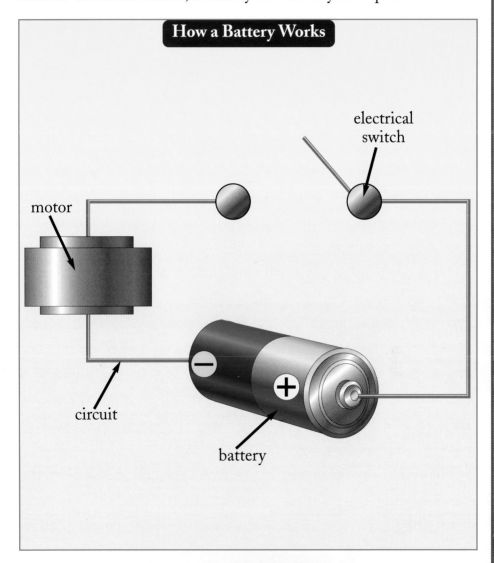

How a Battery Works

electrical switch

motor

circuit

battery

ulb Thermometer

A bulb thermometer can detect and measure changes in temperature. It can measure to tenths of a degree. This is necessary when measuring a human or other animal's body temperature. So, how does a bulb thermometer work?

A bulb thermometer consists of a glass bulb that has temperature marks on it. There is a liquid inside. This is usually mercury, but can sometimes be alcohol. Mercury is more common because it takes a high temperature to make it boil. Alcohol is used mostly in cold environments because it takes a much colder temperature to freeze alcohol.

A bulb thermometer works on the principle that all liquids change when temperature changes. Liquids expand when it is hot and contract when it is cold. So when it is cold, the liquid in a thermometer will contract. This means it will go down the gauge. The opposite happens when it is hot – the liquid expands. This means it goes up the gauge.

The bulb thermometer has many uses. It is used in the manufacturing and medical industries. In the process of melting metal, the precise temperature must be measured. This is because the metal might not melt if the temperature is too low. If the temperature is too high, the property of the metal could change. In medicine, the first clue that someone has an infection is a high body temperature.

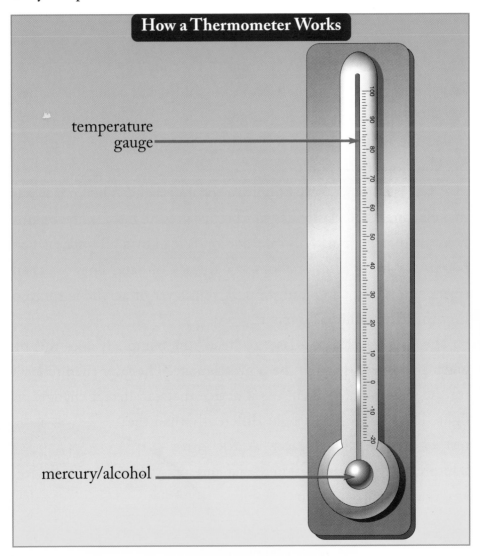

How a Thermometer Works

temperature gauge

mercury/alcohol

ompact Disc

The compact disc, or CD, is a form of technology that is used to store information. This includes music, films, and computer games. A CD is useful because it can store a lot of information. It also makes the information on a disc a lot clearer than other methods. So, how does a CD work?

A CD is a simple piece of polycarbonate plastic. When it is being manufactured, the plastic has tiny bumps pressed into it. The bumps hold the information. This information is read by a CD player. The bumps are arranged in one long spiral track of data. They are then covered in a thin aluminum film. A thin layer of acrylic is sprayed over the aluminum to protect it.

The CD player uses a laser to "read" the bumps. It does this by passing the laser through the polycarbonate. The laser then reflects off the aluminum. It then hits a device that can detect changes in light. The bumps reflect light differently than the rest of the aluminum layer. A disc drive interprets these changes. These changes are what produce music or graphics.

Because CDs are strong, they

have a long lifespan. This means popular games and music do not have to be replaced often.

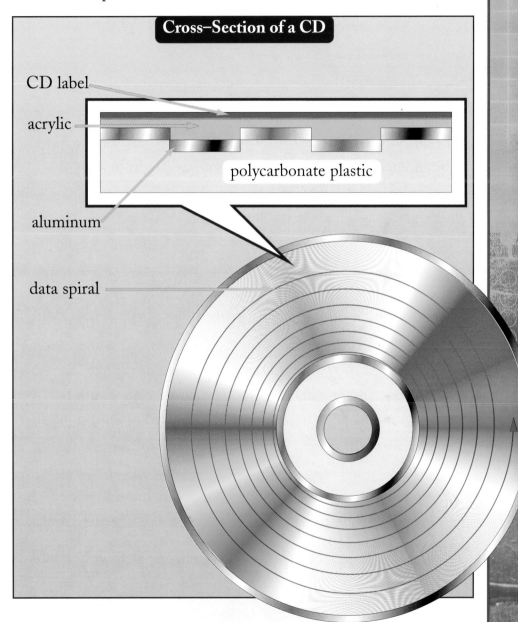

Cross–Section of a CD

CD label

acrylic

polycarbonate plastic

aluminum

data spiral

Electric Light Bulb

The light bulb is a simple invention. A light bulb is a lot safer to use as a light source than gas or an open flame. Its glow can be dimmed or brightened easily. So, how does an electric light bulb work?

Most light bulbs have a glass bulb, electrical contacts, an inert gas, and a filament made of tungsten. Tungsten is a type of metal. When you turn on a light switch, the electrical contacts send electricity to the tungsten filament. The filament heats up rapidly. It becomes white hot. This is the source of the light. Tungsten is used in light bulbs because of its high melting point. Most other metals would melt under such a high heat. An inert gas is used because it stops the white-hot metal from mixing with oxygen. This is needed because oxygen fuels fire. A light bulb would burn out as soon as it came in contact with it.

Electric light bulbs have made changes in the way people live. People do not have to be ruled by night and day. Everyday living has also been made easier. For example, light bulbs are inside ovens and fridges. They also help people work at night or in dark places.

How a Light Bulb Works

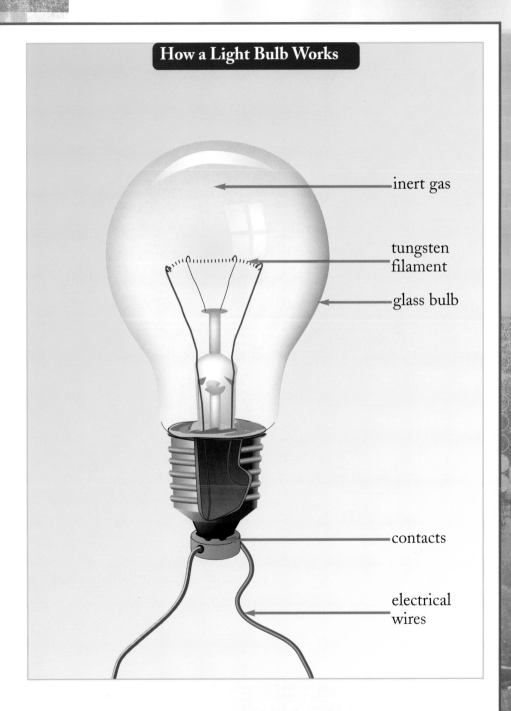

inert gas

tungsten filament

glass bulb

contacts

electrical wires

Helicopter

The helicopter came along about 45 years after the first person flew an aircraft. Developed in the 1940s, helicopters changed the way people thought about flight. No longer did aircraft need a large amount of thrust to take off horizontally. Helicopters could take off and land vertically. So, how does a helicopter work?

A helicopter uses a lot of the same principles as an airplane. An important part of a helicopter is its rotor blades. Like an airplane's wings, the rotor blades are what help it to stay in the air. Each blade of the rotor is shaped like the wing of an airplane. The pilot adjusts the pitch, or angle, of the blade as it spins. This makes the aircraft go up or down. The pilot adjusts the pitch by using the controls inside the cockpit.

The best way to describe the pitch is to imagine having a long piece of wood lying on the ground. If you lift one end of the wood while the other stays on the ground, you have pitch. How high or low you lift the piece of wood determines the pitch. Increasing the pitch makes a helicopter go up in the air. Decreasing the pitch lowers it. The pitch also makes the helicopter hover, go ahead, or move sideways.

Helicopters are used by the military. They are also used in rescue missions. They can be used in hard-to-reach places. Helicopters are slower than most airplanes. They cannot carry as many people or as much cargo. However, they can do things airplanes cannot do. They can hover, move sideways, and in same cases, go in reverse.

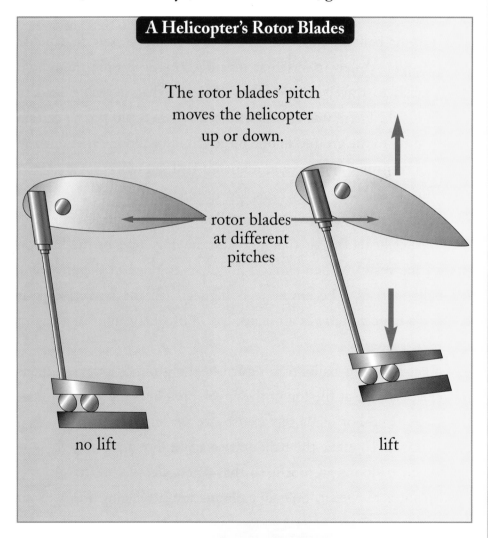

A Helicopter's Rotor Blades

The rotor blades' pitch moves the helicopter up or down.

rotor blades at different pitches

no lift

lift

Hot-Air Balloon

The hot-air balloon was one of the first flying vessels that could carry people. When it was first invented, many people thought it was foolish to travel in one. They thought that it would lead to certain death. There was no way to steer it. You could not be certain of returning to the ground in one piece. Today, balloons are safer and easier to control. So, how does a hot-air balloon work?

A hot-air balloon uses a basic law of science — hot air rises faster than cool air. This is why hot-air balloons have a burner on board. The burner heats the air that is inside the envelope, or the balloon part of the vessel. When enough hot air is trapped in the envelope, the balloon rises. The envelope is bigger than the basket. This is because a large volume of air is needed to lift the weight of a basket and its passengers.

To get a hot-air balloon to return to the ground, a device opens and closes a valve at the top of the envelope. The valve allows hot air to escape. The hot air is replaced by cooler air. The balloon then comes down. To make the balloon rise again, hot air is added.

Hot-air balloons are not used that often. People prefer to travel in airplanes. However, hot-air balloons are a relaxing form of air travel. They glide slowly across the sky. This means they are good for sightseeing trips.

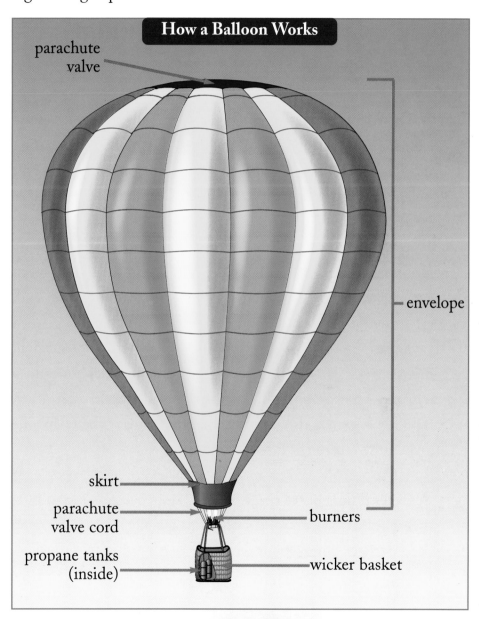

How a Balloon Works

parachute valve

envelope

skirt

parachute valve cord

propane tanks (inside)

burners

wicker basket

Land–Based Telephone

The telephone was invented just over 100 years ago. It is one of the simpler pieces of technology. Its basic operating principles are still in use today. So, how does a telephone work?

A telephone has a microphone in the mouthpiece. It has a loudspeaker in the earpiece. When a person speaks into the mouthpiece, their voice is converted into electrical signals. These signals are sent down wires at a high speed. When the signals reach the loudspeaker on the telephone of the person at the other end, they are turned back into sound.

To make it all work, a hook switch is needed. A hook switch is a small device that connects telephones to a network. The network allows people to telephone each other. The hook switch also connects and disconnects the telephone when the receiver is lifted up or put down.

The telephone has made life easier for most people. It makes it possible to speak to loved ones overseas instantly. It helps people make business decisions quickly instead of having to wait for written correspondence.

How a Telephone Works

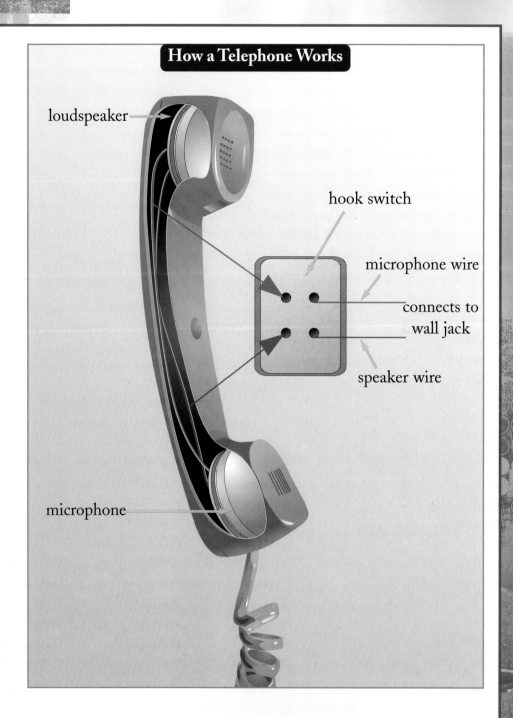

loudspeaker

hook switch

microphone wire

connects to
wall jack

speaker wire

microphone

Microwave Oven

Microwave ovens have become an everyday household item for many people. They can be used to cook or heat up food. They can also defrost food. So, how does a microwave oven work?

Microwaves are radio waves. These radio waves are absorbed by fats, water, and sugar. They are then made into heat. Microwave ovens are good to use because the radio waves heat up only the food or liquid. This is different from a normal oven. A normal oven heats all the surfaces the heat comes in contact with.

Unlike a normal oven, food in a microwave cooks from the inside out. The microwaves excite atoms in the food or beverage being cooked or heated. A fan spreads the microwaves around the oven. In a normal oven, heat is conducted from one part of the food to the next.

There are some problems with using a microwave. Sometimes parts of the food heat up more quickly than others. This is because radio waves penetrate thick pieces of food unevenly. Also, other radio waves can interfere with the microwaves. This also makes the heating of the food or liquid uneven.

A lot of people still like cooking with a normal oven. But

microwave ovens are ideal for busy people who hate the idea of spending a long time cooking a meal. A microwave oven also allows people to reheat food almost instantly. In a normal oven, this can take a lot longer.

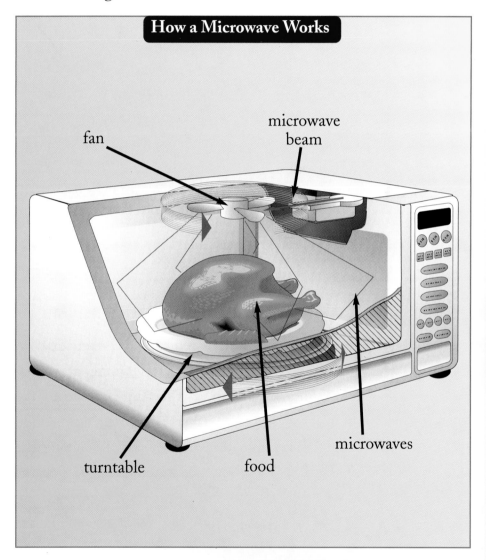

How a Microwave Works

fan

microwave beam

turntable

food

microwaves

Radar

Radar was developed during World War II. It was developed as an early warning system for bombing and fighting aircraft. Since that time radar has changed little. It is used for many things. It can tell the speed of an object. It can help measure the distance to an object. It can also help to map an object. So, how does radar work?

Radar needs two things to work – echo and the Doppler effect. An echo is created when sound waves reflect off a surface. For example, you might shout down a well. The time it takes for a sound wave to leave your mouth, hit a surface, and return to you can be measured. The measurement tells you the distance between you and the surface you are shouting at.

The Doppler effect is when sound is reflected off, or made by, a moving object. For example, imagine a train coming at you at a certain speed. It is sounding its horn. As the train approaches, the horn will be at a certain pitch. When it passes you, the horn sound will be at a different pitch. Even though the horn is making the same sound the whole time, the difference in pitch that you hear is called the Doppler effect. This is because as the train is approaching you, the sound waves are getting shorter. This makes it seem like the horn is making a different sound as it passes you.

Radar uses radio waves, which are invisible. However, they are easy to detect and can travel a long distance. A radar system has a transmitter and receiver. The transmitter sends out short bursts of radio waves at a high frequency. The transmitter then turns itself off and turns on the receiver. The receiver is listening for an echo. The radar then measures the time it takes for the echo to come back. It also measures the Doppler effect of the echo at the same time. The turning on and off of the transmitter and receiver happens quickly. The calculations of time and distance are made in a split second.

Radar allows air-traffic controllers to keep in contact with a large number of aircraft at one time. It helps to make sure that aircraft do not crash into one another while in flight. Most police forces use radar to make sure motorists are keeping within set speed limits. Spacecraft can use radar to map the contours of the Earth. A spacecraft's radar does this by measuring mountains and depressions on the planet's surface.

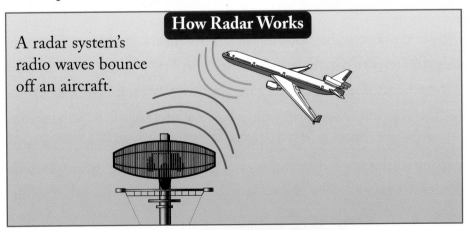

How Radar Works

A radar system's radio waves bounce off an aircraft.

Returning Boomerang

The boomerang started out as a hunting instrument. It was used by the Australian Aborigines. Since then, there have been many variations. One is the returning boomerang. It is designed to come back to the person who throws it. So, how does a returning boomerang work?

Unlike a straight piece of wood, a returning boomerang is made of two pieces of wood, or wings. They are joined together in a banana-like shape. This is the key to it being able to return to you. A central part acts as a stabilizer as it flies through the air.

A boomerang needs lift in order to fly. It gets lift the same way an airplane does. The top part of the boomerang is curved and the bottom part is flat. Air passes over the curved part more quickly than it does over the bottom part. This means there is greater air pressure below than above. This results in lift.

So, how does a boomerang return? When you throw a boomerang, one wing is spinning in the direction of the throw. The other wing is facing the opposite direction. However, it is still moving in the same direction as the other wing. The wing spinning in the direction of the throw is going faster than the other wing.

This makes the boomerang turn left or right. This means it will return to the person who threw it.

Boomerangs are no longer used for hunting. They are sometimes used for fun. There are even worldwide boomerang contests.

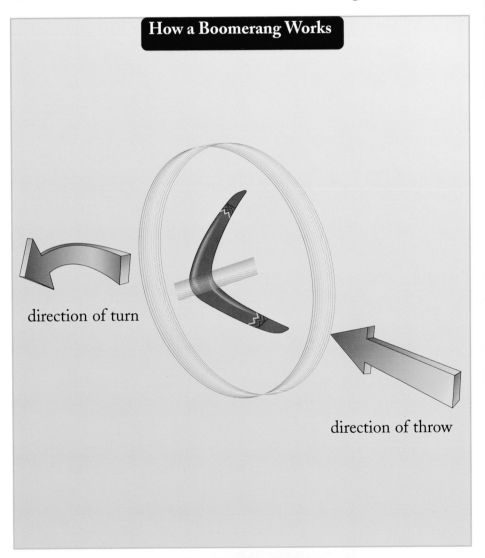

How a Boomerang Works

direction of turn

direction of throw

Telescope

A telescope makes distant objects seem closer. Telescopes help astronomers study the stars. They help ships' captains watch for other ships or obstacles. There are two main types of telescopes – reflector and refractor. Reflector telescopes use mirrors while refractor telescopes use glass lenses. So, how does a telescope work?

The main reason people cannot see distant objects clearly is because of the eye's retina. The retina cannot collect enough light to create a bright image. The retina also cannot magnify the object to "stretch" over the retina. Telescopes have two pieces of equipment that do this. Reflector telescopes have a part called a primary mirror. The primary mirror collects a lot of light from the object that is being observed. The primary mirror brings the object into focus. Refractor telescopes have an item called an objective lens. The objective lens brings the object into focus.

The other piece of equipment telescopes use is called an eyepiece lens. The eyepiece lens takes the light from the focus of the primary mirror or objective lens and magnifies it. When these pieces of equipment are combined, you have a telescope. The telescope then allows you to see objects closer than you can with the naked eye.

Astronomers use powerful telescopes such as the Hubble Telescope, which orbits the Earth. It allows scientists to see things they would not be able to see from Earth. This includes such things as dwarf stars, black holes, and planets in other solar systems in the Milky Way Galaxy.

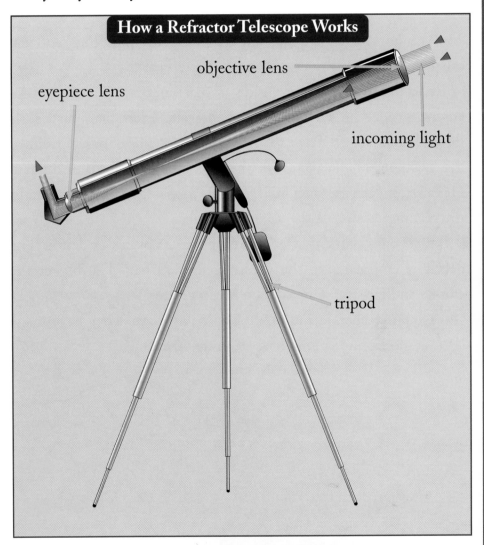

How a Refractor Telescope Works

objective lens

eyepiece lens

incoming light

tripod

Vacuum Cleaner

The vacuum cleaner is a machine that sucks up spills, fluff, and any other dust. But how does a vacuum cleaner work?

Reducing the pressure inside a machine causes suction. An engine inside the vacuum cleaner powers a fan that pushes air through an exhaust. The exhaust can be at the back or the front of the machine. The heaviness of the air increases in front of the fan. However, it decreases behind it. This decrease in air heaviness causes the sucking motion of the vacuum cleaner.

The stream of air that is created picks up pieces of debris. The debris is emptied into the vacuum cleaner's bag. The bigger the engine and fan, the more suction it can create.

Vacuum cleaners come in all shapes and sizes. They have made both domestic and commercial cleaning easier.

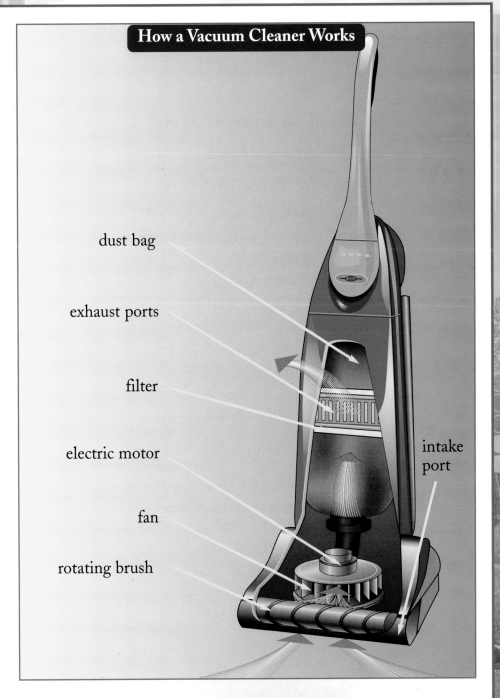

How a Vacuum Cleaner Works

dust bag

exhaust ports

filter

electric motor

fan

rotating brush

intake
port

Glossary

astronomers – Experts who study the universe and all that is in it.

cockpit – The part of an airplane where the pilot sits and flies the vessel.

correspondence – Communicating with someone else, whether it is by e-mail, telephone, letter, or other form of communication.

defrost – When frozen food is left to thaw.

domestic – Anything relating to home or family matters.

electrode – A device that conducts electricity.

interfere – To get in the way of something and stop it from working properly.

portable – Can be moved around easily.

terminal – A point of connection in an electrical circuit.

transmitter – A device that sends out electromagnetic waves.